CONTENTS

COUNTRY OVERVIEW:
ETHIOPIA AT A GLANCE

History

Ethiopia is home to more than 80 ethnic and linguistic communities. Proud to be an African state that was never colonized, the Kingdom of Ethiopia dates back to the first millennium. King Menelik I, the legendary son of Queen Sheba and King Solomon of Israel, established his kingdom in Axum. After the rise of Islam in the seventh century, the kingdom became isolated as Arabs gained control of the Red Sea trading routes. In the 12th century, the successor of the Axumite dynasty had expanded southward, principally to Lalibela.

Ethiopia's modern period (post-1855) was characterized by the process of recreating a cohesive state: by Emperor Haile Selassie; by the Marxist regime of Mengistu Haile Mariam; and, since mid-1991, by the Ethiopian People's Revolutionary Democratic Front (EPRDF) under Meles Zenawi. The period has been dominated by recurring conflict with neighboring Eritrea, which was a province of Ethiopia until it gained independence in 1991. A tentative cease-fire ended hostilities in 2000, but the border remains undefined and tensions continue, particularly since the 2007 withdrawal of U.N. peacekeepers.

Government

In Ethiopia, President Meles Zenawi and members of the Transitional Government of Ethiopia (TGE) pledged to oversee the formation of a multi-party democracy. The election for a 547-member constituent assembly was held in June 1994, and this assembly adopted the constitution of the Federal Democratic Republic of Ethiopia in December 1994. The elections for Ethiopia's first popularly chosen national parliament and regional legislatures were held in May and June 1995. Most opposition parties chose to boycott these elections, ensuring a landslide victory for the EPRDF. International and nongovernmental observers concluded that opposition parties would have been able to participate had they chosen to do so. The Government of the Federal Democratic Republic of Ethiopia was installed in August 1995. Parliament consists of the House of Federation, or upper chamber (108 seats; members are chosen by state assemblies to serve five-year terms), and the House of People's Representatives, or lower chamber (547 seats; members are directly elected by popular vote from single-member districts to serve five-year terms). The Council of Ministers is selected by the prime minister and approved by the House of People's Representatives. The president is elected by the House of People's Representatives for a six-year term (eligible for a second term). The last election was in May 2010; the next will be held in May 2015. The prime minister is designated by the party in power following legislative elections.

Economy

In the economic arena, the TGE inherited a shattered country. In his first public speech after the EPRDF had captured Addis Ababa, Meles Zenawi indicated that Ethiopia's coffers were empty; moreover, some 7 million people were threatened with starvation because of drought and civil war. Economic performance statistics reflected this gloomy assessment.

The current government has embarked on a cautious program of economic reform, including privatization of state enterprises and rationalization of government regulation. While the process is ongoing, reforms have attracted only meager foreign investment.

The Ethiopian economy is based on agriculture, which contributes about 45 percent to gross national product and more than 80 percent of exports, and employs approximately 85 percent of the population. The major agricultural export crop is coffee, providing 35 percent of Ethiopia's foreign exchange earnings, down from 65 percent a decade ago due to a slump in coffee prices since the mid-1990s. Other traditional major agricultural exports are hides and skins, pulses, oilseeds, and leather. Sugar and gold production has also become important in recent years.

Ethiopia's agriculture is plagued by periodic drought, soil degradation caused by poor agricultural practices and overgrazing, deforestation, high population density, undeveloped water resources, and poor transport infrastructure, making it difficult and expensive to get goods to market. Yet agriculture is the country's most promising resource. Potential exists for self-sufficiency in grains and for export development in livestock, flowers, grains, oilseeds, sugar, vegetables, and fruits.

Gold, marble, limestone, and small amounts of tantalum are mined in Ethiopia. Other resources with potential for commercial development include large potash deposits, natural gas, iron ore, and possibly oil and geothermal energy. Although Ethiopia has good hydroelectric resources that power most of its manufacturing sector, it is totally dependent on imports for its oil.

A landlocked country, Ethiopia has relied on the port of Djibouti since the 1998–00 border war with Eritrea. Ethiopia is connected with the port of Djibouti by road and rail for international trade. Of the 23,812 kilometers (14,796 miles) of all-weather roads in Ethiopia, about 7,000 km (4,349 miles) are asphalt. Mountainous terrain and the lack of good roads and sufficient vehicles make land transportation difficult and expensive. However, the government-owned airline's reputation is excellent. Ethiopian Airlines serves 17 domestic airfields and has 62 international destinations.

In November 2001, Ethiopia qualified for debt relief from the Heavily Indebted Poor Countries Initiative, and in 2005 the International Monetary Fund voted to forgive Ethiopia's debt. Under Ethiopia's land tenure system, the government owns all land and provides long-term leases to the tenants; the system continues to hamper growth in the industrial sector as entrepreneurs are unable to use land as collateral for loans.

People and Culture
Ethiopia's population is mainly rural, with most people living in highlands above 5,900 feet (1,800 meters).

Religion plays an important role in Ethiopian society. Almost half the people are Ethiopian Orthodox, while Muslims account for about 35 percent of the total population. A small minority are Catholics or Protestants; the remainder practice traditional religious beliefs. Amharic is the official language at the federal level but there are more than 80 ethnic groups with their own distinct languages within Ethiopia.

Environment

Due to its wide range of altitudes, Ethiopia experiences extremely varied climatic conditions, including cold mountains, temperate highlands, and hot deserts. Normally, the rainy season lasts from mid-June to mid-September (longer in the southern highlands), preceded by intermittent showers from February to May. The remainder of year is generally dry.

RESOURCES FOR FURTHER INFORMATION

Following is a list of websites for additional information about the Peace Corps and Ethiopia and to connect you to returned Volunteers and other invitees. Please keep in mind that although we try to make sure all these links are active and current, we cannot guarantee it. If you do not have access to the Internet, visit your local library. Libraries offer free Internet usage and often let you print information to take home.

A note of caution: As you surf the Internet, be aware that you may find bulletin boards and chat rooms in which people are free to express opinions about the Peace Corps based on their own experience, including comments by those who were unhappy with their choice to serve in the Peace Corps. These opinions are not those of the Peace Corps or the U.S. government, and we hope you will keep in mind that no two people experience their service in the same way.

General Information About Ethiopia

www.countrywatch.com/
On this site, you can learn anything from what time it is in the Addis Ababa to how to convert from the dollar to the Ethiopian birr. Just click on Ethiopia and go from there.

www.lonelyplanet.com/destinations
Visit this site for general travel advice about almost any country in the world.

www.state.gov
The Department of State's website issues background notes periodically about countries around the world. Find **Ethiopia** and learn more about its social and political history. You can also go to the site's international travel section to check on conditions that may affect your safety.

www.psr.keele.ac.uk/official.htm
This includes links to all the official sites for governments worldwide.

www.geography.about.com/library/maps/blindex.htm
This online world atlas includes maps and geographical information, and each country page contains links to other sites, such as the Library of Congress, that contain comprehensive historical, social, and political background.

www.cyberschoolbus.un.org/infonation/info.asp
This United Nations site allows you to search for statistical information for member states of the U.N.

www.worldinformation.com
This site provides an additional source of current and historical information about countries around the world.

Connect With Returned Volunteers and Other Invitees

www.rpcv.org

This is the site of the National Peace Corps Association, made up of returned Volunteers. On this site you can find links to all the Web pages of the "Friends of" groups for most countries of service, comprised of former Volunteers who served in those countries. There are also regional groups that frequently get together for social events and local volunteer activities. Or go straight to the Friends of Ethiopia: http://www.ethiopiaeritrearpcvs.org/.

www.PeaceCorpsWorldwide.org

This site is hosted by a group of returned Volunteer writers. It is a monthly online publication of essays and Volunteer accounts of their Peace Corps service.

Online Articles/Current News Sites About Ethiopia

http://allafrica.com/ethiopia/

News wire stories about Ethiopia

International Development Sites About Ethiopia

http://www.usaid.gov/locations/sub-saharan_africa/countries/ethiopia/

This site explores U.S. Agency for International Development's work in Ethiopia.

Recommended Books

1. Ashabranner, Brent. *A Moment in History: The First Ten Years of the Peace Corps*. Garden City, N.Y.: Doubleday, 1971.

2. Clift, Elayne (ed.). *But Do They Have Field Experience!* Potomac, Md.: OGN Publications, 1993.

3. Kennedy, Geraldine (ed.). *Hartmattan: A Journey across the Sahara*. Santa Monica, Calif.: Clover Park Press, 1991.

4. Mezlekia, Nega. *Hyena's Belly: An Ethiopian Boyhood*, Picador, 2002.

5. Verghesse, Abraham. *Cutting for Stone*. Vintage Canada Edition, 2010.Press, 1991.

Books About the History of the Peace Corps

1. Hoffman, Elizabeth Cobbs. *All You Need is Love: The Peace Corps and the Spirit of the 1960s*. Cambridge, Mass.: Harvard University Press, 2000.

2. Rice, Gerald T. *The Bold Experiment: JFK's Peace Corps*. Notre Dame, Ind.: University of Notre Dame Press, 1985.

3. Stossel, Scott. *Sarge: The Life and Times of Sargent Shriver*. Washington, D.C.: Smithsonian Institution Press, 2004.

4. Meisler, Stanley. *When the World Calls: The Inside Story of the Peace Corps and its First 50 Years*. Boston, Mass.: Beacon Press, 2011.

Books on the Volunteer Experience

1. Dirlam, Sharon. *Beyond Siberia: Two Years in a Forgotten Place*. Santa Barbara, Calif.: McSeas Books, 2004.

2. Casebolt, Marjorie DeMoss. *Margarita: A Guatemalan Peace Corps Experience*. Gig Harbor, Wash.: Red Apple Publishing, 2000.

3. Erdman, Sarah. *Nine Hills to Nambonkaha: Two Years in the Heart of an African Village*. New York, N.Y.: Picador, 2003.

4. Hessler, Peter. *River Town: Two Years on the Yangtze*. New York, N.Y.: Perennial, 2001.

5. Kennedy, Geraldine ed. *From the Center of the Earth: Stories out of the Peace Corps*. Santa Monica, Calif.: Clover Park Press, 1991.

6. Thompsen, Moritz. *Living Poor: A Peace Corps Chronicle*. Seattle, Wash.: University of Washington Press, 1997 (reprint).

LIVING CONDITIONS AND VOLUNTEER LIFESTYLE

Communications

Mail

Few countries in the world offer the level of mail service we take for granted in the United States. Airmail from the United States to major cities in Ethiopia typically takes two to four weeks to arrive. Volunteers have been pleasantly surprised by the efficiency of the Ethiopian postal service, but delayed and lost mail does occur. Advise your family and friends to number their letters and to include "Airmail" and "Par Avion" on their envelopes. Packages normally take three to four weeks to reach Ethiopia via airmail. Flat-rate boxes (available through the United States postal system) are a good deal, allowing the sender to send several things without having to worry about the weight.

Your address during training will be as follows:

Your Name/PCT
U.S. Peace Corps/Ethiopia
P.O. Box 7788
Addis Ababa, Ethiopia

You will purchase a personal postal office box once you move to your site. Mail arriving in Addis Ababa, after you have obtained your own postal office box, will continue to be held at the Peace Corps office until you pass through on official business or when a Peace Corps/Addis Ababa staff member visits you at your site.

Telephones

Almost all sites have telecom centers with international long distance. Peace Corps/Ethiopia provides a telecommunications allowance. Cellular telephones are widespread in Ethiopia, although coverage varies across the country. You will have the option of purchasing a SIM card and phone during pre-service training (PST); all current Volunteers have mobile phones. Volunteers' settling-in allowance includes funds to cover this purchase. For the few Volunteers in extremely remote areas, they are supplemented with a satellite phone from the Peace Corps office for direct communication.

Computer, Internet, and Email Access

Internet access is rapidly changing in Ethiopia. Typically, Internet is available at Internet cafes in many towns and cities, but service can be slow and costly. A growing number of towns now have access to Internet via pre-paid Internet devices (such as CDMA and/or EVDO) that you can purchase in Ethiopia and use with your laptop. During pre-service training, the Peace Corps will provide a small stipend for the CDMA device if your town has access to the CDMA network. As such, several Volunteers are finding it much easier to keep in contact back home. Nevertheless, there are still several sites and Volunteers without access to CDMA, EVDO, or other Internet connection options. You should, therefore, not count on having daily, or even weekly, Internet access during your service in Ethiopia. Designated computers in the resource center at the Peace Corps office have Internet access, and you are welcome to use these when in Addis Ababa or at a Peace Corps regional office. The offices are now equipped with Wi-Fi service exclusively for Volunteers' use. Many Volunteers bring laptops for research, digital photos, or entertainment, but as with any valuable item, there is a risk of theft or damage. Many PCVs recommend bring a laptop computer, but the Peace Corps cannot be held responsible for theft or damage, and you will need to take additional precautions if you choose to bring one.

Housing and Site Location

As a Volunteer, you will most likely live in a peri-urban or small town and have electricity and a water source at your house, although these services suffer frequent outages and shortages. When it comes to your housing, you should not lose sight of the guiding goal of the Peace Corps. Maintain your focus on service to the people of Ethiopia and not on the level of your accommodations.

Housing varies greatly among sites, so the Peace Corps sets minimum housing standards:

- There must be a private, lockable room with a private entrance, if housing is shared with other people.
- The room should have windows.
- The roof should not leak.
- There should be a cement floor and a place for a Volunteer to bathe.
- There should be a bathroom or latrine and shower area that is private with a cemented floor. (*In many cases you will have to share these spaces with others.)
- The Volunteer will use the same water source as those in his or her community.

Your volunteer site assignment is made about halfway into pre-service training (PST) through close collaboration between your Peace Corps project supervisor and the training staff. Site placements are made using the following criteria (in priority order):

- Medical and security considerations
- Priorities of the Ethiopian government
- Site requirements matched with technical, cross-cultural, and language skills of Volunteers
- Personal preference of the trainee expressed during interviews with staff. (Given the limited number of assignment options, you should not expect that your personal preferences will be met for your future site assignment location.)

Living Allowance and Money Management

Each Volunteer receives a monthly allowance sufficient to cover basic costs. The allowance enables Volunteers to live adequately according to the Peace Corps' philosophy of a modest lifestyle. It is based on the local cost of living and is paid in local currency. Your living allowance is intended to cover food, housing, clothing, transportation from home to worksite, utilities, household supplies, recreation and entertainment, incidental personal expenses, and communications.

Food and Diet

In most parts of Ethiopia there is a regular, although limited, selection of fresh fruits and vegetables.

Butcher shops sell beef and lamb, live chickens can be purchased at the market and in areas near lakes, and fresh fish is available. With a little creativity, you can enjoy a varied diet. Fruits and vegetables are seasonal, which means some items may not be available at all times. Vegetarian Volunteers will have little difficulty continuing their diets, as Orthodox Christians "fast" by eating a vegan diet on Wednesdays and Fridays throughout the year. Vegetarianism, however, is not common, so be prepared to explain your habits. Meat is eaten during special occasions and holidays, so it may be prudent to discuss your vegetarianism with host families early to avoid embarrassing or offending them.

Transportation

All Volunteers will be expected to travel in Ethiopia using local transportation (i.e., foot, bicycle, public buses, and minivans—called "line taxis"). Volunteers may not own or operate motorized vehicles in Ethiopia. The Peace Corps will provide a stipend for Volunteers wishing to purchase a bike (with helmet) at their site. If you purchase a bike, you are required to always wear a helmet while riding.

Geography and Climate

Most of Ethiopia is tropical due to its proximity to the equator, but since most of the country's land mass is above 4,920 feet (1,500 meters), the climate is not what many normally associate with the tropics. Ethiopia experiences extremely varied climatic conditions from cool or very cold in the highlands, which most of the population inhabits, to one of the hottest places on Earth, the Danakil Depression.

Social Activities

The most common form of entertainment is socializing among friends and neighbors. Some Volunteers visit other Volunteers on weekends and holidays. The Peace Corps encourages Volunteers to remain at their sites as much as possible to develop relationships with community members, but it also recognizes that they need to make occasional trips to regional centers and to visit friends.

You will find it easy to make friends in your community and to participate in weddings, funerals, birthday celebrations, holiday celebrations, and other social events. It is impossible to overemphasize the rewards of establishing rapport with supervisors, co-workers, and other community members. A sincere effort to learn the local language will greatly facilitate these interactions.

Professionalism, Dress, and Behavior

Ethiopians regard dress and appearance as an outward sign of the respect one holds for another individual. Neatness in appearance is more important than being "stylish." Volunteers should always wear clean and neat clothes. Buttoned shirts for men and blouses and pants, skirts, or dresses (to or below the knee) for women are appropriate during business hours. T-shirts are appropriate only for casual, non-business activities. Tank tops, see-through blouses, and low-cut blouses are not appropriate; exposing one's shoulders is unacceptable. Blue jeans should not be worn during business hours unless the conditions of the job assignment or training activity allow it, and never when visiting government offices. Shorts may be worn only at home, when exercising (if appropriate).

Aside from dress, there are other standards of appearance that must be respected. Women should wear appropriate undergarments, including bras and slips. Your hair should be clean and combed. For men, beards should be neatly trimmed.

The matter of sexual behavior is, of course, a highly personal one. However, because of other social implications of such behavior, it is important that Peace Corps standards be clear. Sexual mores in Ethiopia are very conservative and strict, and you are expected to respect them. Public displays of affection between members of the opposite sex, such as kissing, hand holding, or hugging are not generally socially acceptable, though hand holding among men is very common. Homosexual and indecent acts are illegal in Ethiopia and punishable by imprisonment or deportation. Further information will be provided during your PST on appropriate and inappropriate sexual behavior.

These restrictions have been formalized in response to specific instances of inappropriate dress and behavior by Volunteers. In general, the above guidance is meant to convey to Volunteers that adherence to professional standards is appropriate at all times and in all places. When in doubt, look to your Ethiopian counterparts for guidance. If the country director determines that willful disregard of cultural standards is jeopardizing your credibility or that of the program, you may be administratively separated from the Peace Corps.

Personal Safety

More detailed information about the Peace Corps' approach to safety is contained in the Health Care and Safety chapter, but it is an important issue and cannot be overemphasized. As stated in the Volunteer Handbook, becoming a Peace Corps Volunteer entails certain safety risks. Living and traveling in an unfamiliar environment (oftentimes alone), having a limited understanding of local language and culture, and being perceived as well-off are some of the factors that can put a Volunteer at risk. Many Volunteers experience varying degrees of unwanted attention and harassment. Petty thefts and burglaries are not uncommon, and incidents of physical and sexual assault do occur, although most Ethiopia Volunteers complete their two years of service without incident. The Peace Corps has established procedures and policies designed to help you reduce your risks and enhance your safety and security. These procedures and policies, in addition to safety training, will be provided once you arrive in Ethiopia. Using these tools, you are expected to take responsibility for your safety and well-being.

Each staff member at the Peace Corps is committed to providing Volunteers with the support they need to successfully meet the challenges they will face to have a safe, healthy, and productive service. Volunteers and families are encouraged to look at the safety and security information on the Peace Corps website at **www.peacecorps.gov/safety**.

Information on these pages gives messages on Volunteer health and Volunteer safety. There is a section titled Safety and Security—Our Partnership. Among topics addressed are the risks of serving as a Volunteer, posts' safety support systems, and emergency planning and communications.

Rewards and Frustrations

Before accepting this assignment, you should give ample thought to some of the potential obstacles you will face. Until you adjust to living in Ethiopia, you will undoubtedly feel out of place speaking a new language and trying to practice customs that may seem strange to you. No matter what your ethnic, religious, or racial background is, you may stick out as someone from outside the Ethiopian culture. However, many situations can be overcome with a sense of humor and an open mind.

Your work situation will also present many difficulties and frustrations. Most of your work will be to educate, motivate, and organize community groups, often a slow task. You will find yourself in situations that require an ability to motivate yourself and your community to take action with little guidance from your colleagues and counterparts. You must possess the self-confidence, patience, and vision to continue working toward long-term goals without seeing immediate results or feedback. Co-workers, severely underpaid and burdened with extended family commitments, will have a much different outlook on life than your own. Rainy and agricultural seasons, as well as vacations and holidays, will delay and threaten the "success" of many project activities. As each Volunteer's job description will be uniquely dependent upon the expressed needs of the community and the skills that you bring, you will be constantly defining and redefining your role as you attempt to meet the needs of your community. This is both a gift and a challenge: a gift in that you are free to work in areas where you are needed most and really make a difference in your community, and a challenge in that you must invent and reinvent yourself in an oftentimes unstructured work environment. Defining your role and finding your niche within your community will be one of your greatest challenges. You may have to reach beyond your assigned counterpart and organizations to find people and opportunities to begin projects. This aspect of your work will be difficult, but can be achieved with time, personal drive, resourcefulness, and a flexible and patient mind. And who knows, you may meet some great people in the process!

Peace Corps service is not for everyone. More than a job, it requires greater dedication and commitment to serve than do most other work environments. It is for confident, self-starting, and concerned individuals who are interested in assisting in other countries and increasing understanding across cultures. It is for those who can laugh at themselves, who can be spontaneous, and who can step far outside of their comfort zone. If you have the personal qualities needed to accept the challenges described above and can demonstrate them for a two-year service commitment in Ethiopia, you will have a rewarding, enriching, and lasting experience, while at the same time making a much-needed contribution to the development of Ethiopia.

Even with the many economic, social, political, and environmental challenges facing Ethiopia today, there is an atmosphere of excitement and hope. The changes occurring in health, environment, education, and infrastructure development are some of the most important in the country's modern history. To join the people of Ethiopia in this effort, and to be part of this historic defining moment, will be both fascinating and satisfying to Volunteers willing to work hard, be tolerant, and give generously of their time.

PEACE CORPS TRAINING

Pre-Service Training

PST will be busy for everyone. Often you will work more than eight hours a day before returning to your host family in the evening. Be prepared for a rigorous and full schedule. Training will be conducted by Ethiopian staff members and current Volunteers who will serve as valuable resources for dealing with the many questions that will arise. PST covers five major topics:

Technical Training

Technical training will prepare you to work in Ethiopia by building on the skills you already have and helping you develop new skills in a manner appropriate to the needs of the country. The Peace Corps staff, Ethiopia experts, and current Volunteers will conduct the training program. Training places great emphasis on learning how to transfer the skills you have to the community in which you will serve as a Volunteer.

Technical training will include sessions on the general economic and political environment in Ethiopia and strategies for working within such a framework. You will review your technical sector's goals and will meet with the Ethiopian agencies and organizations that invited the Peace Corps to assist them. You will be supported and evaluated throughout the training to build the confidence and skills you need to undertake your project activities and be a productive member of your community.

Language Training

As a Peace Corps Volunteer, you will find that language skills are key to personal and professional satisfaction during your service. These skills are critical to your job performance, they help you integrate into your community, and they can ease your personal adaptation to the new surroundings. Therefore, language training is at the heart of the training program. You must successfully meet minimum language requirements to complete training and become a Volunteer. Ethiopia language instructors teach formal language classes five days a week in small groups of four to five people.

Your language training will incorporate a community-based approach. In addition to classroom time, you will be given assignments to work on outside of the classroom and with your host family. The goal is to get you to a point of basic social communication skills so you can practice and develop language skills further once you are at your site. Prior to being sworn in as a Volunteer, you will work on strategies to continue language studies during your service.

Cross-Cultural Training

As part of your pre-service training, you will live with a Ethiopian host family. This experience is designed to ease your transition to life at your site. Families go through an orientation conducted by Peace Corps staff to explain the purpose of pre-service training and to assist them in helping you adapt to living in Ethiopia. Many Volunteers form strong and lasting friendships with their host families.

Cross-cultural and community development training will help you improve your communication skills and understand your role as a facilitator of development. You will be exposed to topics such as community mobilization, conflict resolution, gender and development, nonformal and adult education strategies, and political structures.

Health Training

During pre-service training, you will be given basic medical training and information. You will be expected to practice preventive health care and to take responsibility for your own health by adhering to all medical policies. Trainees are required to attend all medical sessions. The topics include preventive health measures and minor and major medical issues that you might encounter while in Ethiopia. Nutrition, mental health, setting up a safe living compound, and how to avoid HIV/AIDS and other sexually transmitted infections (STIs) are also covered.

Safety Training

During the safety training sessions, you will learn how to adopt a lifestyle that reduces your risks at home, at work, and during your travels. You will also learn appropriate, effective strategies for coping with unwanted attention and about your individual responsibility for promoting safety throughout your service.

Additional Trainings During Volunteer Service

In its commitment to institutionalize quality training, the Peace Corps has implemented a training system that provides Volunteers with continual opportunities to examine their commitment to Peace Corps service while increasing their technical and cross-cultural skills. During service, there are usually three training events. The titles and objectives for those trainings are as follows:

- In-service training: *Provides an opportunity for Volunteers to upgrade their technical, language, and project development skills while sharing their experiences and reaffirming their commitment after having served for three to six months.*

- Midterm conference (done in conjunction with technical sector in-service): *Assists Volunteers in reviewing their first year, reassessing their personal and project objectives, and planning for their second year of service.*

- Close-of-service conference: *Prepares Volunteers for the future after Peace Corps service and reviews their respective projects and personal experiences.*

The number, length, and design of these trainings are adapted to country-specific needs and conditions. The key to the training system is that training events are integrated and interrelated, from the pre-departure orientation through the end of your service, and are planned, implemented, and evaluated cooperatively by the training staff, Peace Corps staff, and Volunteers.

YOUR HEALTH CARE AND SAFETY IN ETHIOPIA

The Peace Corps' highest priority is maintaining the good health and safety of every Volunteer. Peace Corps medical programs emphasize the preventive, rather than the curative, approach to disease. The Peace Corps in Ethiopia maintains a clinic with a full-time medical officer, who takes care of Volunteers' primary health-care needs. Additional medical services, such as testing and basic treatment, are also available in Ethiopia at local hospitals. If you become seriously ill, you will be transported either to an American-standard medical facility in the region or to the United States.

Health Issues in Ethiopia

Ethiopia is geographically diverse. Health risks in Ethiopia include insect-borne diseases such as malaria, tick-borne typhus, and dengue fever; food- and water-borne diseases such as intestinal worms, giardiasis, amebiasis, typhoid fever, and hepatitis A and E, cholera; and hepatitis B, HIV/AIDS, polio, rabies, and snake bites. There are also periodic outbreaks of meningococcal meningitis in some areas. Schistosomiasis is also very common.

Helping You Stay Healthy

The Peace Corps will provide you with all the necessary inoculations, medications, and information to stay healthy. Upon your arrival in Ethiopia, you will receive a medical handbook. At the end of training, you will receive a medical kit with supplies to take care of mild illnesses and first aid needs. The contents of the kit are listed later in this chapter.

During pre-service training, you will have access to basic medical supplies through the medical officer. However, you will be responsible for your own supply of prescription drugs and any other specific medical supplies you require, as the Peace Corps will not order these items during training. Please bring a three-month supply of any prescription drugs you use, since they may not be available here and it may take several months for shipments to arrive.

You will have physicals at midservice and at the end of your service. If you develop a serious medical problem during your service, the medical officer in Ethiopia will consult with the Office of Medical Services (OMS) in Washington, D.C. If it is determined that your condition cannot be treated in Ethiopia, you may be sent out of the country for further evaluation and care.

Maintaining Your Health

As a Volunteer, you must accept considerable responsibility for your own health. Proper precautions will significantly reduce your risk of serious illness or injury. The adage "An ounce of prevention is worth a pound of cure" becomes extremely important in areas where diagnostic and treatment facilities are not up to the standards of the United States. The most important of your responsibilities in Ethiopia is to take the following preventive measures:

Many illnesses that afflict Volunteers worldwide are entirely preventable if proper food and water precautions are taken. These illnesses include food poisoning, parasitic infections, hepatitis A, dysentery, Guinea worms, tapeworms, and typhoid fever. Your medical officer will discuss specific standards for water and food preparation in Ethiopia during pre-service training.

You are taking risks if you choose to be sexually active. To lessen risk, use a condom every time you have sex. Whether your partner is a host country citizen, a fellow Volunteer, or anyone else, do not assume this person is free of HIV/AIDS or other STIs. You will receive more information from the medical officer about this important issue.

Volunteers are expected to adhere to an effective means of birth control to prevent an unplanned pregnancy. Your medical officer can help you decide on the most appropriate method to suit your individual needs. Contraceptive methods are available without charge from the medical officer.

It is critical to your health that you promptly report to the medical office or other designated facility for scheduled immunizations, and that you let the medical officer know immediately of significant illnesses and injuries.

Women's Health Information

Pregnancy is treated in the same manner as other Volunteer health conditions that require medical attention but also have programmatic ramifications. The Peace Corps is responsible for determining the medical risk and the availability of appropriate medical care if the Volunteer remains in-country. Given the circumstances under which Volunteers live and work in Peace Corps countries, it is rare that the Peace Corps' medical and programmatic standards for continued service during pregnancy can be met.

If feminine hygiene products are not available for you to purchase on the local market, the Peace Corps medical officer in Ethiopia will provide them. If you require a specific product, please bring a three-month supply with you.

Your Peace Corps Medical Kit

The Peace Corps medical officer will provide you with a kit that contains basic items necessary to prevent and treat illnesses that may occur during service. Kit items can be periodically restocked at the medical office.

Medical Kit Contents

Ace bandages

Adhesive tape

American Red Cross First Aid & Safety Handbook

Antacid tablets (Tums)

Antibiotic ointment (Bacitracin/Neomycin/Polymycin B)

Antiseptic antimicrobial skin cleaner (Hibiclens)

Band-Aids

Butterfly closures

Calamine lotion

Cepacol lozenges

Condoms

Dental floss

Diphenhydramine HCL 25 mg (Benadryl)

Insect repellent stick (Cutter)

Iodine tablets (for water purification)

Lip balm (Chapstick)

Oral rehydration salts

Oral thermometer (Fahrenheit)

Pseudoephedrine HCL 30 mg (Sudafed)

Robitussin-DM lozenges (for cough)

Scissors

Sterile gauze pads

Tetrahydrozaline eyedrops (Visine)

Tinactin (antifungal cream)

Tweezers

Before You Leave: A Medical Checklist

If there has been any change in your health—physical, mental, or dental—since you submitted your examination reports to the Peace Corps, you must immediately notify OMS. Failure to disclose new illnesses, injuries, allergies, or pregnancy can endanger your health and may jeopardize your eligibility to serve.

If your dental exam was done more than a year ago, or if your physical exam is more than two years old, contact OMS to find out whether you need to update your records. If your dentist or Peace Corps dental consultant has recommended that you undergo dental treatment or repair, you must complete that work and make sure your dentist sends requested confirmation reports or X-rays to OMS.

If you wish to avoid having duplicate vaccinations, contact your physician's office to obtain a copy of your immunization record and bring it to your pre-departure orientation. If you have any immunizations prior to Peace Corps service, the Peace Corps cannot reimburse you for the cost. The Peace Corps will provide all the immunizations necessary for your overseas assignment, either at your pre-departure orientation or shortly after you arrive in Ethiopia. You do not need to begin taking malaria medication prior to departure.

Bring a three-month supply of any prescription or over-the-counter medication you use on a regular basis, including birth control pills. Although the Peace Corps cannot reimburse you for this three-month supply, it will order refills during your service. While awaiting shipment—which can take several months—you will be dependent on your own medication supply. The Peace Corps will not pay for herbal or nonprescribed medications, such as St. John's wort, glucosamine, selenium, or antioxidant supplements.

You are encouraged to bring copies of medical prescriptions signed by your physician. This is not a requirement, but they might come in handy if you are questioned in transit about carrying a three-month supply of prescription drugs.

If you wear eyeglasses, bring two pairs with you. If a pair breaks, the Peace Corps will replace them, using the information your doctor in the United States provided on the eyeglasses form during your examination. The Peace Corps discourages you from using contact lenses during your service to reduce your risk of developing a serious infection or other eye disease. Most Peace Corps countries do not have appropriate water and sanitation to support eye care with the use of contact lenses. The Peace Corps will not supply or replace contact lenses or associated solutions unless an ophthalmologist has recommended their use for a specific medical condition and OMS has given approval.

If you are eligible for Medicare, are over 50 years of age, or have a health condition that may restrict your future participation in health-care plans, you may wish to consult an insurance specialist about unique coverage needs before your departure. The Peace Corps will provide all necessary health care from the time you leave for your pre-departure orientation until you complete your service. When you finish, you will be entitled to the post-service health care benefits described in the Peace Corps Volunteer Handbook. You may wish to consider keeping an existing health plan in effect during your service if you think age or pre-existing conditions might prevent you from re-enrolling in your current plan when you return home.

Safety and Security—Our Partnership

Serving as a Volunteer overseas entails certain safety and security risks. Living and traveling in an unfamiliar environment, a limited understanding of the local language and culture, and the perception of being a wealthy American are some of the factors that can put a Volunteer at risk. Property theft and burglaries are not uncommon. Incidents of physical and sexual assault do occur, although almost all Volunteers complete their two years of service without serious personal safety problems.

Beyond knowing that Peace Corps approaches safety and security as a partnership with you, it might be helpful to see how this partnership works. Peace Corps has policies, procedures, and training in place to promote your safety. We depend on you to follow those policies and to put into practice what you have learned. An example of how this works in practice—in this case to help manage the risk of burglary—is as follows:

- Peace Corps assesses the security environment where you will live and work

- Peace Corps inspects the house where you will live according to established security criteria

- Peace Corps provides you with resources to take measures such as installing new locks

- Peace Corps ensures you are welcomed by host country authorities in your new community

- Peace Corps responds to security concerns that you raise

- You lock your doors and windows

- You adopt a lifestyle appropriate to the community where you live

- You get to know neighbors

- You decide if purchasing personal articles insurance is appropriate for you

- You don't change residences before being authorized by Peace Corps

- You communicate concerns that you have to Peace Corps staff

Factors that Contribute to Volunteer Risk

There are several factors that can heighten a Volunteer's risk, many of which are within the Volunteer's control. By far the most common crime that Volunteers experience is theft. Thefts often occur when Volunteers are away from their sites, in crowded locations (such as markets or on public transportation), and when leaving items unattended.

Before you depart for Ethiopia there are several measures you can take to reduce your risk:

- Leave valuable objects in the U.S.

- Leave copies of important documents and account numbers with someone you trust in the U.S.

- Purchase a hidden money pouch or "dummy" wallet as a decoy

- Purchase personal articles insurance

After you arrive in Ethiopia, you will receive more detailed information about common crimes, factors that contribute to Volunteer risk, and local strategies to reduce that risk. For example, Volunteers in Ethiopia learn to do the following:

- Choose safe routes and times for travel, and travel with someone trusted by the community whenever possible

- Make sure one's personal appearance is respectful of local customs

- Avoid high-crime areas

- Know the local language to get help in an emergency

- Make friends with local people who are respected in the community

- Limit alcohol consumption

As you can see from this list, you must be willing to work hard and adapt your lifestyle to minimize the potential for being a target for crime. As with anywhere in the world, crime does exist in Ethiopia. You can reduce your risk by avoiding situations that place you at risk and by taking precautions. Crime at the village or town level is less frequent than in the large cities; people know each other and generally are less likely to steal from their neighbors. Tourist attractions in large towns are favorite worksites for pickpockets.

The following are other security concerns in Ethiopia of which you should be aware:

- Verbal harassment and unwanted attention;
- Theft, pick-pocketing and "snatch and run," especially in cities;

- Transportation-related accidents.

While whistles and exclamations may be fairly common on the street, this behavior can be reduced if you dress conservatively, abide by local cultural norms, and respond according to the training you will receive.

Staying Safe: Don't Be a Target for Crime

You must be prepared to take on a large degree of responsibility for your own safety. You can make yourself less of a target, ensure that your home is secure, and develop relationships in your community that will make you an unlikely victim of crime. While the factors that contribute to your risk in Ethiopia may be different, in many ways you can do what you would do if you moved to a new city anywhere: Be cautious, check things out, ask questions, learn about your neighborhood, know where the more risky locations are, use common sense, and be aware. You can reduce your vulnerability to crime by integrating into your community, learning the local language, acting responsibly, and abiding by Peace Corps policies and procedures. Serving safely and effectively in Ethiopia will require that you accept some restrictions on your current lifestyle.

Some prevention techniques you will learn in PST that will help keep you safer and to avoid the more common concerns in Ethiopia include the following:

- Developing very good community integration skills, working with children and parents.
- For women, identifying other women with whom you can work, travel, and spend time with who will help you mitigate unwanted attention.
- Not carrying large amounts of money or material valuables (such as electronics or jewelry).
- Learning common warning signs for theft in Ethiopia, such as distraction techniques.
- Learning to use Peace Corps-approved transportation methods and avoiding certain risky transportation situations.
- Becoming accustomed to traveling in groups, especially at night.

Support from Staff

If a trainee or Volunteer is the victim of a safety incident, Peace Corps staff is prepared to provide support. All Peace Corps posts have procedures in place to respond to incidents of crime committed against Volunteers. The first priority for all posts in the aftermath of an incident is to ensure the Volunteer is safe and receiving medical treatment as needed. After assuring the safety of the Volunteer, Peace Corps staff response may include reassessing the Volunteer's worksite and housing arrangements and making any adjustments, as needed. In some cases, the nature of the incident may necessitate a site or housing transfer. Peace Corps staff will also assist Volunteers with preserving their rights to pursue legal sanctions against the perpetrators of the crime. It is very important that Volunteers report incidents as they occur, not only to protect their peer Volunteers, but also to preserve the future right to prosecute. Should Volunteers decide later in the process that they want to proceed with the prosecution of their assailant, this option may no longer exist if the evidence of the event has not been preserved at the time of the incident.

Crime Data for Ethiopia

Crime data and statistics for Ethiopia, which is updated yearly, are available at the following link: http://www.peacecorps.gov/countrydata/ethiopia. Please take the time to review this important information.

Few Peace Corps Volunteers are victims of serious crimes and crimes that do occur overseas are investigated and prosecuted by local authorities through the local courts system. If you are the victim of a crime, you will decide if you wish to pursue prosecution. If you decide to prosecute, the Peace Corps will be there to assist you. One of our tasks is to ensure you are fully informed of your options and understand how the local legal process works. The Peace Corps will help you ensure your rights are protected to the fullest extent possible under the laws of the country.

If you are the victim of a serious crime, you will learn how to get to a safe location as quickly as possible and contact your Peace Corps office. It's important that you notify Peace Corps staff as soon as you can so the Peace Corps can provide you with the help you need.

Volunteer Safety Support in Ethiopia

The Peace Corps' approach to safety is a five-pronged plan to help you stay safe during your service and includes the following: information sharing, Volunteer training, site selection criteria, a detailed emergency action plan, and protocols for addressing safety and security incidents. Ethiopia's in-country safety program is outlined below.

The Peace Corps/Ethiopia office will keep you informed of any issues that may impact Volunteer safety through *information sharing*. Regular updates will be provided in Volunteer newsletters and in memorandums from the country director. In the event of a critical situation or emergency, you will be contacted through the emergency communication network. An important component of the capacity of Peace Corps to keep you informed is your buy-in to the partnership concept with the Peace Corps staff. It is expected that you will do your part in ensuring that Peace Corps staff members are kept apprised of your movements in-country so they are able to inform you.

Volunteer training will include sessions on specific safety and security issues in Ethiopia. This training will prepare you to adopt a culturally appropriate lifestyle and exercise judgment that promotes safety and reduces risk in your home, at work, and while traveling. Safety training is offered throughout service and is integrated into the language, cross-cultural aspects, health, and other components of training. You will be expected to successfully complete all training competencies in a variety of areas, including safety and security, as a condition of service.

Certain *site selection criteria* are used to determine safe housing for Volunteers before their arrival. The Peace Corps staff works closely with host communities and counterpart agencies to help prepare them for a Volunteer's arrival and to establish expectations of their respective roles in supporting the Volunteer. Each site is inspected before the Volunteer's arrival to ensure placement in appropriate, safe, and secure housing and worksites. Site selection is based, in part, on any relevant site history; access to medical, banking, postal, and other essential services; availability of communications, transportation, and markets; different housing options and living arrangements; and other Volunteer support needs.

You will also learn about Peace Corps/Ethiopia's *detailed emergency action plan,* which is implemented in the event of civil or political unrest or a natural disaster. When you arrive at your site, you will complete and submit a site locator form with your address, contact information, and a map to your house. If there is a security threat, you will gather with other Volunteers in Ethiopia at predetermined locations until the situation is resolved or the Peace Corps decides to evacuate.

Finally, in order for the Peace Corps to be fully responsive to the needs of Volunteers, it is imperative that Volunteers immediately report any security incident to the Peace Corps office. The Peace Corps has established ***protocols for addressing safety and security incidents*** in a timely and appropriate manner, and it collects and evaluates safety and security data to track trends and develop strategies to minimize risks to future Volunteers.

DIVERSITY AND
CROSS-CULTURAL ISSUES

In fulfilling its mandate to share the face of America with host countries, the Peace Corps is making special efforts to assure that all of America's richness is reflected in the Volunteer corps. More Americans of color are serving in today's Peace Corps than at any time in recent history. Differences in race, ethnic background, age, religion, and sexual orientation are expected and welcomed among our Volunteers. Part of the Peace Corps mission is to help dispel any notion that Americans are all of one origin or race and to establish that each of us is as thoroughly American as the other despite our many differences.

Our diversity helps us accomplish that goal. In other ways, however, it poses challenges. In Ethiopia, as in other Peace Corps host countries, Volunteers' behavior, lifestyle, background, and beliefs are judged in a cultural context very different from their own. Certain personal perspectives or characteristics commonly accepted in the United States may be quite uncommon, unacceptable, or even repressed in Ethiopia.

Outside of Ethiopia's capital, residents of rural communities have had relatively little direct exposure to other cultures, races, religions, and lifestyles. What people view as typical American behavior or norms may be a misconception, such as the belief that all Americans are rich and have blond hair and blue eyes. The people of Ethiopia are justly known for their generous hospitality to foreigners; however, members of the community in which you will live may display a range of reactions to cultural differences that you present.

To ease the transition and adapt to life in Ethiopia, you may need to make some temporary, yet fundamental compromises in how you present yourself as an American and as an individual. For example, female trainees and Volunteers may not be able to exercise the independence available to them in the United States; political discussions need to be handled with great care; and some of your personal beliefs may best remain undisclosed. You will need to develop techniques and personal strategies for coping with these and other limitations. The Peace Corps staff will lead diversity and sensitivity discussions during pre-service training and will be on call to provide support, but the challenge ultimately will be your own.

Overview of Diversity in Ethiopia

The Peace Corps staff in Ethiopia recognizes the adjustment issues that come with diversity and will endeavor to provide support and guidance. During PST, several sessions will be held to discuss diversity and coping mechanisms. We look forward to having male and female Volunteers from a variety of races, ethnic groups, ages, religions, and sexual orientations, and hope that you will become part of a diverse group of Americans who take pride in supporting one another and demonstrating the richness of American culture.

What Might a Volunteer Face?

Possible Issues for Female Volunteers

Peace Corps Volunteers in Ethiopia work mostly in rural areas. Traditional gender roles are very distinct in Ethiopia. Generally, women are expected to show deference to men and do most of the housework. Sexual harassment (e.g., men making unwanted comments) is common. The safety of our female Volunteers is of the utmost importance; female Volunteers are encouraged to live vigilantly and take necessary precautions. The loss of freedom to go wherever you please whenever you please has proven to frustrate many Volunteers. Female Volunteers should expect curiosity from host country friends regarding their marital status and whether they have children, and if not, why.

Possible Issues for Volunteers of Color

The average rural Ethiopian assumes that all Americans are white (Caucasian). White Volunteers may receive special attention, both positive and negative, including being harassed for money or food, especially in public areas. Some Ethiopians are unaware that there are black, Asian, and Latino Americans, and may not believe, at first, that you are an American.

Volunteers of color in Ethiopia will have unique experiences and encounters with issues related to their race and ethnicity. In the United States, Volunteers may identify themselves as a member of a specific group and in Ethiopia they may suddenly find themselves being labeled "white," "China," or "Kenya." This may contribute to a Volunteer feeling frustrated and compel him/her to prove who they are or manage emotions of confrontation.

Possible Issues for Senior Volunteers

The Ethiopian culture has great respect for age. As a senior Volunteer, people may offer to do things for you as a sign of respect. Since the mandatory retirement age is 55, Ethiopians may not fully comprehend why a "retiree" would still be working.

Pre-service training may be physically demanding for older Volunteers. Likewise, language acquisition may also be challenging.

Because most Peace Corps Volunteers are comparatively young, older Volunteers may feel a sense of isolation within the Volunteer community. On the other hand, older Volunteers may serve as mentors and be sought out by the younger Volunteer community.

Possible Issues for Married Couple Volunteers

Married Volunteers have the support of one another, which can oftentimes alleviate the stress of daily life in Ethiopia. However, they may face other challenges. Sometimes, one spouse may be more enthusiastic about joining the Peace Corps and, therefore, more willing to adapt to the challenges of living in a new culture. One spouse may also learn the language quicker than the other, causing the potential for friction.

Married Volunteers may be expected by community members to uphold entrenched Ethiopian cultural gender roles. A married man might be encouraged to be the more dominant member of the family, make independent decisions, and have his wife serve him. He may also be ridiculed if he performs domestic tasks. A married woman might find herself in a less independent role with a more limited social life in the community than single female Volunteers. She may also be expected to perform "traditional' domestic chores, such as housekeeping or child rearing.

The normal bumps in the road that are a part of any close, intense relationship, such as marriage, are unlikely to have the same set of normal outlets and networks as at home. This lack of release, like a pressure cooker, can help "cook the problem thoroughly" much quicker. Married Volunteers should feel at ease with the Peace Corps medical officer and married staff members to discuss the pressures of married Volunteer life.

Possible Issues for Gay, Lesbian, or Bisexual Volunteers

Homosexual acts are illegal in Ethiopia and are punishable by imprisonment or deportation. Many Ethiopians have beliefs about homosexuality similar to those of many Americans in the 1940s and 1950s. It is important for gay, lesbian, or bisexual Volunteers to know about these conservative attitudes to be able to live and work productively in Ethiopian communities. Past Volunteers in Ethiopia have reported that they could not publicly acknowledge their sexual orientation for fear of negative repercussions. We suggest that anyone wishing to discuss this subject do so in confidence with a Peace Corps staff member. The medical office can provide confidential counseling and help connect you with the gay and lesbian support group for returned Volunteers.

A recommended resource for support and advice prior to and during your service is the Lesbian, Gay, Bisexual, and Transgender U.S. Peace Corps Alumni website at **www.lgbrpcv.org.**

Possible Religious Issues for Volunteers

Volunteers may face many questions in regard to their religion and spiritual views. This can be quite an adjustment for Volunteers since religion is considered a private matter in the U.S. Religion in Ethiopia is markedly different; it is public and often a topic of conversation that is discussed freely. The most prevalent religion is Christianity, Orthodox and Protestant, followed by Islam.

It is not considered rude to ask a person about his or her religion. You will find that during most conversations with host country nationals it is one of the first questions you will be asked after your name, nationality, and occupation.

Possible Issues for Volunteers With Disabilities

As part of the medical clearance process, OMS determined that you were physically and emotionally capable, with or without reasonable accommodations, to perform a full tour of Volunteer service in Ethiopia without unreasonable risk of harm to yourself or interruption of service. The Peace Corps/Ethiopia staff will work with disabled Volunteers to make reasonable accommodations for them in training, housing, jobsites, or other areas to enable them to serve safely and effectively. The post complies with the Americans With Disabilities Act to ensure productive Peace Corps service by physically challenged Volunteers. Ethiopians who are physically challenged are generally not accorded the same human dignity as other Ethiopians. Regardless of the nature of the physical challenge, social services are generally lacking for these Ethiopians. Ethiopia has little infrastructure to accommodate the needs of individuals with physical handicaps, blindness, or mobility impairment.

FREQUENTLY ASKED QUESTIONS

This list has been compiled by Volunteers serving in Ethiopia and is based on their experience. Use it as an informal guide in making your own list, bearing in mind that each experience is individual. There is no perfect list! You obviously cannot bring everything on the list, so consider those items that make the most sense to you personally and professionally. You can always have things sent to you later. As you decide what to bring, keep in mind that you have a 100-pound weight limit on baggage. And remember, you can get almost everything you need in Ethiopia.

How much luggage am I allowed to bring to Ethiopia?
Most airlines have baggage size and weight limits and assess charges for transport of baggage that exceeds those limits. The Peace Corps has its own size and weight limits and will not pay the cost of transport for baggage that exceeds these limits. The Peace Corps' allowance is two checked pieces of luggage with combined dimensions of both pieces not to exceed 107 inches (length + width + height) and a carry-on bag with dimensions of no more than 45 inches. Checked baggage should not exceed 100 pounds total with a maximum weight of 50 pounds for any one bag.

Peace Corps Volunteers are not allowed to take pets, weapons, explosives, radio transmitters (shortwave radios are permitted), automobiles, or motorcycles to their overseas assignments. Do not pack flammable materials or liquids such as lighter fluid, cleaning solvents, hair spray, or aerosol containers. This is an important safety precaution.

What is the electric current in Ethiopia?
The local current is 220-240 volts/50 cycles. Small electrical appliances can generally be used with converters. Most electronic equipment (MP3 players, battery chargers, etc.) will operate on local current with just an adapter (two small round pins).

How much money should I bring?
Volunteers are expected to live at the same level as the people in their community. You will be given a settling-in allowance and a monthly living allowance, which should cover your expenses. Volunteers often wish to bring additional money for vacation travel to other countries. Credit cards and traveler's checks are preferable to cash. If you choose to bring extra money, bring the amount that will suit your own travel plans and needs.

When can I take vacation and have people visit me?
Each Volunteer accrues two vacation days per month of service (excluding training). Leave may not be taken during training, the first three months of service, or the last three months of service, except in conjunction with an authorized emergency leave. Family and friends are welcome to visit you after pre-service training and the first three months of service as long as their stay does not interfere with your work. Extended stays at your site are not encouraged and may require permission from your country director. The Peace Corps is not able to provide your visitors with visa, medical, or travel assistance.

Will my belongings be covered by insurance?
The Peace Corps does not provide insurance coverage for personal effects; Volunteers are ultimately responsible for the safekeeping of their personal belongings. However, you can purchase personal property insurance before you leave. If you wish, you may contact your own insurance company; additionally, insurance application forms will be provided, and we encourage you to consider them carefully. Volunteers should not ship or take valuable items overseas. Jewelry, watches, radios, cameras, and expensive appliances are subject to loss, theft, and breakage, and in many places, satisfactory maintenance and repair services are not available.

Do I need an international driver's license?

Volunteers in Ethiopia do not need an international driver's license because they are prohibited from operating privately owned motorized vehicles. Most urban travel is by bus or taxi. Rural travel ranges from buses and minibuses to trucks, bicycles, and lots of walking. On very rare occasions, a Volunteer may be asked to drive a sponsor's vehicle, but this can occur only with prior written permission from the country director. Should this occur, the Volunteer may obtain a local driver's license. A U.S. driver's license will facilitate the process, so bring it with you just in case.

What should I bring as gifts for Ethiopia friends and my host family?

This is not a requirement. A token of friendship is sufficient. Some gift suggestions include knickknacks for the house; pictures, books, or calendars of American scenes; souvenirs from your area; hard candies that will not melt or spoil; or photos to give away.

Where will my site assignment be when I finish training and how isolated will I be?

Peace Corps trainees are not assigned to individual sites until after they have completed pre-service training. This gives Peace Corps staff the opportunity to assess each trainee's technical and language skills prior to assigning sites, in addition to finalizing site selections with their ministry counterparts. If feasible, you may have the opportunity to provide input on your site preferences, including geographical location, distance from other Volunteers, and living conditions. However, keep in mind that many factors influence the site selection process and that the Peace Corps cannot guarantee placement where you would ideally like to be. Most Volunteers live in small towns or in rural villages and are usually within one hour from another Volunteer. Some sites require a 10- to 12-hour drive from the capital.

How can my family contact me in an emergency?

The Peace Corps Counseling and Outreach Unit (COU) provides assistance in handling emergencies affecting trainees and Volunteers or their families. Before leaving the United States, instruct your family to notify COU immediately if an emergency arises, such as a serious illness or death of a family member. During normal business hours, the number for COU is 855.855.1961, then select option 2; or directly at 202-692-1470. After normal business hours and on weekends and holidays, the COU duty officer can be reached at the above number. For non-emergency questions, your family can get information from your country desk staff at the Peace Corps by calling 855.855.1961.

Can I call home from Ethiopia?

Yes, but calls can be expensive and Skype can be very erratic. It is suggested that Volunteers and friends and family members individually investigate long distance calling cards and plans, as these rates and services are constantly changing.

Should I bring a cellular phone with me?

You should discontinue the use of your cell phone plan as most likely you will not have international calling access from Ethiopia. You will need to purchase an Ethiopian SIM card with the help of the Peace Corps. If you choose to bring your cell phone from the United States, be aware that 3G Internet technology is only beginning to be developed in Ethiopia. Smartphones also bring unwanted attention so you may wish to leave these at home and purchase a "less flashy" cellphone in Ethiopia.

Will there be email and Internet access?
Should I bring my computer?

Internet service in Ethiopia is slow and erratic compared to the U.S. Wireless access is to the Internet is rarely available and often not secure.

Many Volunteers decide to bring laptops and external hard drives to Ethiopia and, by and large, are glad they did. However, there is always the possibility it could get lost, stolen, or damaged, and repair parts are often difficult to obtain locally or expensive.

WELCOME LETTERS FROM ETHIOPIA VOLUNTEERS

Greetings, *ferenji* (foreigner)! Welcome to Ethiopia!

Congratulations on successfully completing the long and tedious application process and obtaining the coveted invitation letter!

What is life like in Ethiopia? Boy, I wish I could answer that! Each experience is unique. What I can say is that it will be full of adventure, embarrassing moments, challenging experiences, and rewarding outcomes. When you first get here your hands will probably shake from all of the coffee you drink. After about two months, you will develop an unnaturally high tolerance for caffeine. You will live with a host family that will constantly tell you to eat, even if you have food in your mouth.

Children with snot running from their noses will run up to you with big smiles on their faces and shake your hands. People will stop whatever they are doing to watch you walk across the street, buy food from the market, or pick up a piece of paper you dropped. You will get used to seeing sheep and goats tied to the top of minivans. After about three months, your eyes will not bulge out as they cram 30 people in a minivan built for 12.

Eventually, you will be able to walk confidently to the marketplace and know how to ask the lady for a kilo of potatoes. One day, you will have a big goofy smile on your face because you finally understood what the *suk* (store) owner said to you. You will build relationships with people that will touch you deeply. You will be inspired by the people and their kind hearts. You will make a difference in people's lives, even though you may never see it.

But, before you head to the motherland, I would like to offer a few words of advice and encouragement. Not too long ago, I remember receiving the list of suggested items to pack sent by the Volunteers. I tried to fit every single one of those things in my bags, which led me to have four extremely heavy bags. I ended up having to leave two bags worth of clothes, blankets, and junk that I didn't need (including a pair of heels). Pay attention to airline weight limits! You can always pack a box in the States and have it shipped to you. Just bring the things that you absolutely need now, and would be devastated to live without.

Initially, I was completely nervous when I received my invitation. I am serving as an environmental Volunteer, but I have a business background, with limited experience in the environmental sector. You may be nervous about how you will use your expertise with your assignment. But don't worry! The Peace Corps placement officers gave you this assignment because they know that your skills can be used and are greatly needed. Each Volunteer has a different skill set, and each community has its own needs. They will also give you technical skills training to enhance your skill set. I am using my business background to help farmers develop environment-friendly income-generating activities and teaching farmers' wives basic business concepts.

Remember that you are here not only to share your talent, but to learn about Ethiopian culture and to share your own culture. Take time to participate in cultural events, greet your neighbors, and develop relationships. Ethiopians are very welcoming and will appreciate any attempt you make to talk to them. They will invite you to their homes, host coffee ceremonies for you, hold your hand while they show you around town, and ask you to break bread with them. Please don't be afraid to make a fool of yourself. You won't be the first *ferenji* to do so. During the first week of training, one of my fellow Volunteers tried to tell her host mother that she loves egg sandwiches, but instead she told them she "loves butt sandwiches." It created a bond between her and her host mother—a memory for them to cherish.

Remember to laugh when you find yourself in these types of situations. Have fun! *Gorsha* your host mom (a cultural practice of shoving food in someone's mouth), drink seven cups of coffee a day, play soccer with the kids, take the time to learn the language, and share your experiences with loved ones back home.

You will also have a wonderful support network of your peers ready to help you. Don't be afraid to ask us any questions (including how to use the *shint bet*/latrine).

Environment Volunteer in Tigray Region

....

Selam Naw!

On behalf of all the current Volunteers here in Ethiopia, allow me to congratulate you on embarking on a remarkable journey to the birthplace of coffee and the cradle of civilization. Many things and beings got their start here, including the Peace Corps (Ethiopia was one of the very first countries to request PCVs in 1962). Hardly a day goes by without an elder telling me, proudly, "I was taught by a Peace Corps Volunteer." As such, Ethiopia welcomes American Volunteers with open arms.

In thinking of your service in Ethiopia you may have imagined dry, dusty wastelands, a starving population, and nomadic tribes warring over cattle—but it's far from the reality here. Ethiopia is, in many ways, unlike any other country in Africa, and you will be enthralled at the diversity. Where I live in Western Ethiopia there's dense tropical rainforest. Other PCVs are scattered in the rocky highlands of the north, the flat scrubland of the Rift Valley, the chilly mountains of Bale or Simiens, or the cosmopolitan flair of Ethiopia's regional capitals. While the food here is amazing, you can always reliably fall back on peanut butter and banana sandwiches, even in the smaller towns.

No matter your site, it will get colder at night and the rainy season brings its own kinds of challenges. Bring jeans, a jacket, thermals, and a durable raincoat. The two things Ethiopians maintain the most is their hair and their shoes, so bring nice work shoes and consider a haircut. While you aren't going on a two-year camping trip, oftentimes it will feel like you're living out of a backpack. Pack versatile clothes that you could wear again and again and again with minimal washing. Dress smart. Ethiopians appreciate it.

Start practicing your patience and flexibility now, as these will be your greatest strengths in weathering the adaptation to a culture that makes plans on-the-fly, places special emphasis on greetings, and uses an entirely different clock and calendar than the West. These concepts are second nature to me now, but at first blush they had the power to turn my usual calm, collected self into a bag of rants. Don't worry: You will adjust. Everything will be fine.

Leaving behind beloved family and friends in the U.S. for over two years is probably the hardest part about the Peace Corps, but you will soon realize that you're joining a PCV family here in Ethiopia. We are a natural support group willing to help your transition to Ethiopia go as smoothly as possible. As awkward as we were in the beginning, my PST group has now become old friends I can count on after a period of distress. So launch a Facebook group and start the conversation as soon as you can.

A few words for the Education Volunteers: You will be picking up a new program and running very, very far with it. English language teacher training and its many facets may be overwhelming at first, but plenty of lessons were learned in the first group and we are now ready to prepare you to hit the ground running. Don't leave the U.S. without a reliable laptop, small portable speakers, software installation media, external hard drives, an e-reader, and a handful of flash drives. Try to fail-safe everything, as electronics and a bumpy dusty Africa often clash.

The most important thing in the months before you depart for staging is to absorb as much American culture, food, and sports events as you can. If there's one thing you'll walk away with as a PCV, it's a deeper understanding and appreciation of the American way of life, in all its chaotic, epic grandeur. Moreover, be ready for daily surprises here in Ethiopia. One day you might miss cheese, but the next day you'll crave *injera* (spongy sour bread). One day 100 kids shouting at you will drain you while the next an Ethiopian's big wide smile will floor you. Expect the unexpected, and you're well on your way.

Fare forward, travelers!

Education Volunteer in Southern Nations Region

....

> *"There are a few things harder to put up with than*
> *a good example."* —Mark Twain

Dear future Volunteers,

I couldn't agree more with the famous words of Mark Twain. When I arrived in Ethiopia several months ago I did not know what to expect in terms of how I'd be received. Different emotions went through my mind, similar to the feelings you are probably feeling now: Anxiety about whether I'd be able to set the right example and how much effort it was all really going to take. Slowly but surely, I've been able to get to know the Ethiopian people and have realized they are more similar than different. At the end of the day, they all want the same things we do: the best for themselves, their families, and their communities. The relationships I've built have encouraged me to forge forward and work toward our common goals of sustainability and mutual benefit.

As you prepare to embark upon your service in Ethiopia, I encourage you to plan to do the same. Get to know the people in your community. Build relationships and make friendships. Learn about their lives, their families, and their goals. Remember to be proactive and that if you want to make impact, that impact begins with you. There will be times you will feel frustrated, but remember, no matter how hard you try, you can't fall further than from where you began. As you grow as an individual and in your respective community, know that with each attempt of your positive efforts you will achieve more confidence in yourself as well as be successful in your assignment.

Arrive with an open mind and an ideal for service to the town you will be assigned. As you commence, acknowledge and attempt to understand the culture and the values of the Ethiopian people. Most importantly, always remember that the good example you set goes a long way in shaping this society, as well as yourself.

Health Volunteer in Amhara Region

....

Congratulations and welcome to the Peace Corps/Ethiopia family!

If you've never been to Ethiopia before, then you've never been anywhere like Ethiopia. You will have at least two years to experience it, and you will still be seeing new things at the end of your stay. You might be placed in a hot lowland city or a small alpine village, working with international NGOs or just the members of your community. You will learn at least one language and possibly a smattering of several, adjust to not having a winter, set your watch to Ethiopia's own time, and learn the best spots for coffee, and when there is electricity and when there isn't. If nothing else, you will have good local food and coffee wherever you go. Welcome to a two-year learning experience. Be patient!

One of the remarkable features of Ethiopia is its diversity, not only in culture and language, but also in development, altitude, terrain, and vegetation. Pack clothes for hot and cold weather, and make up two boxes for someone at home to mail out upon request: one consisting of hot weather clothes and one with cool weather clothes. Since there is no way to know where you'll end up before you get here, it is best to make preparations for both extremes. In either case, pack things you like and clothes you will be comfortable wearing. Dress respectfully, but realize that you're still going to stand out.

The Peace Corps proudly calls a Volunteer's work "the hardest job you'll ever love," and that is often true, but not necessarily because you'll be working hard. In fact, for many Volunteers, finding work in the beginning is often the hardest part of the job. The daily challenges of finding and making food, getting around, braving curious crowds, and trying to work with people who often seem ambivalent to your very presence will be more wearing than you expect. The Peace Corps is also sometimes known as "the hardest job you'll never understand," and that is also often true. The work you accomplish here often will not sound much like work when you try to describe it to folks back home, and even to you it may be difficult to know what you are accomplishing until after it is over. Just being you, a foreigner, living in your site will have greater ripple effects than you can initially appreciate, so take your time. You will accomplish what you will accomplish, even if you can't describe it very well and even if you're never sure what the lasting impact will be.

Because your work life and your daily life will merge and overlap, be prepared to spend your free time in a way that is valuable and productive, to you if to no one else. You'll spend a lot of time cooking, but you'll also have time for other pursuits. If you read, bring books (but there are also a lot here among PCVs to share). If you write, bring notebooks. If you paint or draw, bring your materials. If you like to juggle or slackline, bring those things.

Share what you do with your community, even if it is just reading in a café. They will want to spend time with you, no matter how or when. Remember that being you is part of your job, so do it well and be prepared for a lot of spectators, no matter what you're doing. You will be the most interesting thing in your town when you first arrive, and you'll probably still be the most interesting thing in your town when you leave, so accept it. The faster you can adjust to being the center of constant attention, the more comfortable you'll be.

There is an interesting duality to being a foreigner *("ferenji")* here. Ethiopia never had the colonizing influence that most other African nations had, so foreigners are still quite novel in most places. People will be very friendly and open with you, curious to ask questions, but they will also shout out to/at you on the street for no apparent reason. Some people will go out of their way to give you special treatment, while others (much more rarely) will go out of their way to try and shake you down. Children will be endlessly fascinated by everything you do, and that fascination will sometimes seem adorable and sometimes seem like harassment. Just get used to it. This, too, is part of your new job.

No matter where you end up, whether it is Tigray or Oromiya, you can and will find your place. Be patient with yourself and your community and life will gradually be what you make of it. This is one amazing journey and no two are alike. So take the time you need to mentally adjust to Ethiopia and remember to come in with minimal expectations. You will be successful. But remember, Western standards of success and accomplishment are just one way to measure success.

Welcome!

Environment Volunteers in Oromiya Region

PACKING LIST

This list has been compiled by Volunteers serving in Ethiopia and is based on their experience. Use it as an informal guide in making your own list, bearing in mind that each experience is individual. There is no perfect list! You obviously cannot bring everything on the list, so consider those items that make the most sense to you personally and professionally. You can always have things sent to you later. As you decide what to bring, keep in mind that you have an 100-pound weight limit on baggage. And remember, you can get almost everything you need in Ethiopia.

General Clothing

Bring clothing that makes you feel good, but still works with Ethiopian dress standards. You will find that clothing you bring from home will suffer more wear and tear than usual, so don't bring anything you will be sad to see ruined. Most Ethiopians wear the same outfit for several days and you will probably adopt that same practice. Also, Ethiopians are pretty thin people, so finding clothes in-country can be difficult. Height is different too.

Some suggestions:

- rain jacket
- scarves
- bandanas
- sunglasses
- jeans
- hiking socks
- bathing suit
- long skirt (mid-calf at least)
- warm tights/spandex for under skirts
- good hat
- work pants
- T-shirts for lounging/working
- lightweight workout/sport pants
- lightweight, quick-dry apparel
- nice pants, black slacks
- button-down shirts

Shoes

Durable shoes are essential. Shoes will wear out more quickly in Ethiopia because of all the walking you will do. Sizes run small so most American sizes are not available.

- hiking shoes (ankle height)
- mud/rain boots (especially if larger than size-10 male)
- light hiking shoe/day shoe

- sandals/Chacos/Keens/Crocs
- slippers
- running shoes
- dressy flats

Personal Hygiene and Toiletry Items

Most basic hygiene items are available, but selection is limited. The Peace Corps provides a medical kit with first aid supplies, insect repellent, sun screen, and over-the-counter medications. Also consider the following:

- face wash
- razors
- facial sun block (if you have sensitive skin)
- tweezers
- shampoo
- hand mirror
- anti-bacterial hand soap (small for travel)
- contacts
- cotton swabs
- saline
- a few toothbrushes
- deodorant
- hair cutting scissors
- diva cup (women)
- tampons (women)

Recreation/Entertainment

Though pre-service training will be very busy, you may find yourself with a great deal of free time when you might have to entertain yourself once you are in your worksite, particularly at night. Bring your favorite hobbies or materials to learn new ones, such as the following:

- camera
- shortwave radio/iPod/music player
- laptop (you will want this)
- small laptop speakers
- external hard drive for movies, podcasts, etc.
- USB drive
- headlamp
- key chain flashlight

- headphones
- crank-powered flashlight
- anti-virus software for PC computer
- rechargeable batteries and charger
- power converter
- sewing kit
- compass
- stationary
- list of addresses for writing snail mail
- index cards for language
- good pens/notebooks
- earplugs
- photo album of family/friends
- exercise videos
- jump rope
- Frisbee
- soccer ball
- yoga mat
- cards
- games
- travel board games (such as Bananagrams/Scrabble)
- Super glue
- clinometer
- work gloves
- seeds
- binoculars
- camping gear
- musical instrument

*   **An important note on surge protectors:** It is a very good idea to run your computer and other electronic items through a surge protector, as currency fluctuates drastically and often in Ethiopia. Surge protectors are, however, voltage specific, so a U.S. 110-volt surge protector will not work in Ethiopia. (In fact, it will blow as soon as you plug it in.) 220-volt surge protectors are available in Ethiopia; although, their quality is not high. An alternative to purchasing a 220-volt surge protector in Ethiopia would be to buy one in the U.S. from a company specializing in 220-volt products. There are several of these companies online.

Kitchen/Household Items

Most kitchenware/household items can be found in the capital or other big cities. However, the first couple of months are not spent in these cities. Some useful items include the following:

- good kitchen knife
- spatula
- can opener
- veggie peeler
- zip-close bags
- small frying pan/sauce pan
- water bottle
- French press
- travel mug
- spices (your favorites—consider black pepper and garlic salt!)
- gum/candy
- multi-tool/pocketknife
- small screwdriver set, glasses repair
- duct tape
- pack of ultra-absorbent towels
- fitted sheet
- sleeping bag
- masking or clear tape
- umbrella

Miscellaneous
- host family gift
- solar shower
- travel wallet
- travel locks for luggage
- weeklong trip pack
- big duffel
- school/small backpack, messenger bag
- tote

*   **Note:** Again, bring those items you feel you cannot live without. Items that make you feel good should also be packed.

PRE-DEPARTURE CHECKLIST

The following list consists of suggestions for you to consider as you prepare to live outside the United States for two years. Not all items will be relevant to everyone, and the list does not include everything you should make arrangements for.

Family

- Notify family that they can call COU at any time if there is a critical illness or death of a family member (24-hour telephone number: 855.855.1961, then press 2, then ext. 1470; or directly at 202.692.1470).

- Give the Peace Corps' *On the Home Front* handbook to family and friends.

Passport/Travel

- Forward to the Peace Corps travel office all paperwork for the Peace Corps passport and visas.

- Verify that your luggage meets the size and weight limits for international travel.

- Obtain a personal passport if you plan to travel after your service ends. (Your Peace Corps passport will expire three months after you finish your service, so if you plan to travel longer, you will need a regular passport.)

Medical/Health

- Complete any needed dental and medical work.

- If you wear glasses, bring two pairs.

- Arrange to bring a three-month supply of all medications (including birth control pills) you are currently taking.

Insurance

- Make arrangements to maintain life insurance coverage.

- Arrange to maintain supplemental health coverage while you are away. (Even though the Peace Corps is responsible for your health care during Peace Corps service overseas, it is advisable for people who have pre-existing conditions to arrange for the continuation of their supplemental health coverage. If there is a lapse in coverage, it is often difficult and expensive to be reinstated.)

- Arrange to continue Medicare coverage if applicable.

Personal Papers

- Bring a copy of your certificate of marriage or divorce.

Voting

- Register to vote in the state of your home of record. (Many state universities consider voting and payment of state taxes as evidence of residence in that state.)

- Obtain a voter registration card and take it with you overseas.

- Arrange to have an absentee ballot forwarded to you overseas.

Personal Effects

- Purchase personal property insurance to extend from the time you leave your home for service overseas until the time you complete your service and return to the United States.

Financial Management

- Keep a bank account in your name in the U.S.

- Obtain student loan deferment forms from the lender or loan service.

- Execute a Power of Attorney for the management of your property and business.

- Arrange for deductions from your readjustment allowance to pay alimony, child support, and other debts through the Office of Volunteer Financial Operations at 855.855.1961 ext. 1770.

- Place all important papers—mortgages, deeds, stocks, and bonds—in a safe deposit box or with an attorney or other caretaker.

CONTACTING PEACE CORPS HEADQUARTERS

This list of numbers will help connect you with the appropriate office at Peace Corps headquarters to answer various questions. You can use the toll-free number and extension or dial directly using the local numbers provided. Be sure to leave the toll-free number and extensions with your family so they can contact you in the event of an emergency.

Peace Corps Headquarters toll-free number: 855.855.1961, press 1 or the extension number (see below)

Peace Corps mailing address: Peace Corps Headquarters
1111 20th Street, NW
Washington, DC 20526

For Questions About:	Staff:	Toll-Free Ext.	Direct/Local Number
Responding to an Invitation:	Office of Placement	ext. 1840	202.692.1840
Country Information:	Patrick Koster Desk Officer /Ethiopia, Malawi, Namibia Ethiopia@peacecorps.gov	ext. 2323	202.692.2323
Plane Tickets, Passports, Visas, or other travel matters:			
	CWT SATO Travel	ext. 1170	202.692.1170
Legal Clearance:	Office of Placement	ext. 1840	202.692.1840
Medical Clearance and Forms Processing (includes dental):			
	Screening Nurse	ext. 1500	202.692.1500
Medical Reimbursements (handled by a subcontractor):			800.818.8772
Loan Deferments, Taxes, Financial Operations:		ext. 1770	202.692.1770
Readjustment Allowance Withdrawals, Power of Attorney, Staging (Pre-Departure Orientation), and Reporting Instructions:			
	Office of Staging	ext. 1865	202.692.1865

Note: You will receive comprehensive information (hotel and flight arrangements) three to five weeks prior to departure. This information is not available sooner.

Family Emergencies (to get information to a Volunteer overseas) *24 hours*:			
	Counseling & Outreach Unit	ext. 1470	202.692.1470

www.ingramcontent.com/pod-product-compliance
Lightning Source LLC
Chambersburg PA
CBHW041518280526
45792CB00004B/1290